White Rose, Red Rose

White Rose, Red Rose

Haiku
by
JOHNNY BARANSKI
& DAVID H. ROSEN

RESOURCE *Publications* • Eugene, Oregon

WHITE ROSE, RED ROSE

Resource Publications
An Imprint of Wipf and Stock Publishers
199 W. 8th Ave., Suite 3
Eugene, OR 97401

www.wipfandstock.com

PAPERBACK ISBN: 978-1-5326-4440-5
HARDCOVER ISBN: 978-1-5326-4441-2
EBOOK ISBN: 978-1-5326-4442-9

Manufactured in the U.S.A.   12/11/17

Cover Art © by Diane Katz

To the Memory of Heather Heyer

Preface

It's difficult to talk about freedom without falling into such clichés as "freedom's just another word for nothin' left to lose. . ." (from "Me and Bobby McGee" by Kris Kristofferson) or freedom is responsibility, or freedom isn't free. For me freedom is more like jazz improvisation. I remember having a conversation with Cor Van den Heuvel, American haiku poet and editor of The Haiku Anthology (Norton 1999), about syllable count in haiku at the Haiku North America conference in Seattle some years ago. As far as he was concerned syllable count in haiku was irrelevant. Once he was inspired he would simply let the poem take him wherever it led whether comprised of seventeen syllables, two syllables, or twenty-four syllables. Improvisation. This little book of forty haiku, twenty each by David Rosen and myself, is about freedom, improvisation, like jazz riffs between sax and trumpet.

> because it is
> the right thing to do
> white rose

—Johnny Baranski, September 2017

Haiku for me started in the sixth grade when schools in Springfield, Missouri integrated due to the U. S. Supreme Court ruling in Brown v. Board of Education. Mrs. Murphy used the "simple" 5-7-5 format to teach her pre-Junior High students how to become haiku poets. This, perhaps, was common practice or ought to have been. Nevertheless, a haiku seed was planted and since has grown into a flowering haiku tree. My haiku habit was thoroughly nurtured decades later by Robert Spiess, editor of *Modern Haiku*. While we never met, he's the best haiku editor I have ever known, although Vincent Tripi and Robert Epstein rank right up there with him. How wonderful it is that haiku has evolved over the years. Now we have the freedom to say what we want in only a few syllables.

> Heather Heyer
> holding a red rose,
> died for peace

—David Rosen, September 2017

Acknowledgements

SOME OF THESE POEMS first appeared in *Acorn, Bones, Cattails, Modern Haiku, Prune Juice, Psychological Perspectives, Seed Packets, Spring, The Heron's Nest,* and *tinywords.com.*

orange is
the new black
marigolds

—JB

Gold is
eternal. . .
Mary, too

    —DR

short timers
in the prison yard
mayflies

    —JB

Crimson foxglove
pierces
field of dry grass

  —DR

up to my eyeballs
in busy work
dragonfly

—JB

Sitting in the rain
waiting for the train
to nowhere

—DR

a train whistle
fades in the moonlight
mountain snow

       —JB

Can it be
I'm falling in love again
with Nature?

       —DR

ebb tide
no closer to you
than the moon

      —JB

Pond side—
suddenly a
glistening turtle

—DR

a pop foul
plops
in the frog pond

     —JB

She is all you need
make love
not war

  —DR

shooting star
another wish
MIA

   —JB

You see me
I see you. . .
praying mantis

—DR

cold snap!
we have
words

       —JB

Tree watching
I see a bird. . .
memories of childhood

—DR

empty nest
Bird and his horn
keep me company

—JB

Numb,
arching vulture
soars

    —DR

unicorns and dragons
take to the sky
kite festival

— JB

Tree pruning,
deer
in the night

— DR

off and on
the stone lantern
firefly

— JB

lonely haiku hut
fireflies
lead the way

— DR

Indian Summer sky . . .
tomahawk
cruise missiles

— JB

Shadow burnt into wall—
rain falls, leaving no sound
behind

— DR

angels have descended
upon the earth
first snow

— JB

Belated
honeymoon—
the rest of my life

— DR

her short-lived
walk down the aisle. . .
damselfly

— JB

Holding hands
our age spots
kiss

— DR

he said
she said
two autumns

— JB

Sin city—
thunder or gunfire
in the distance

— DR

bullet points
on gun control
Orion's Belt

      —JB

Dawn on a spring sea—
then a glittering
from a thousand jumping fish

—DR

all alone on this beach
I too am
but a grain of sand

—JB

Red maple leaves
scattered on moss—
sound of falling water

—DR

white supremacist
his obituary
doesn't mention it

    —JB

Dr. Nada is my name—
my card
nothing on it

     —DR

the ex-con
starts a new life. . .
fireweed

—JB

No
mind—
cleaning the birdbath

—DR

Coltrane
the old jalopy
hums along

— JB

Lavender blooms
outside the sanctuary—
late summer rain

— DR

www.ingramcontent.com/pod-product-compliance
Lightning Source LLC
Chambersburg PA
CBHW071744020426
42331CB00008B/2166